THE OHIO STATE® UNIVERSITY COOKBOOK

JEN ELSNER AND JULIE METZLER

PHOTOGRAPHS BY ZAC WILLIAMS

GIBBS SMITH

TO ENRICH AND INSPIRE HUMANKIND

First Edition
17 16 15 14 13   5 4 3 2 1

Published by
Gibbs Smith
P.O. Box 667
Layton, Utah 84041

1.800.835.4993 orders
www.gibbs-smith.com

Designed by Melissa Dymock
Printed and bound in China

Gibbs Smith books are printed on either recycled, 100% post-consumer
waste, FSC-certified papers or on paper produced from sustainable
PEFC-certified forest/controlled wood source. Learn more at www.pefc.org.

Library of Congress Cataloging-in-Publication Data

Elsner, Jen.
The Ohio State University cookbook / Jen Elsner and Julie Metzler;
photographs by Zac Williams. — First edition.
pages cm
ISBN 978-1-4236-3458-4
1. Outdoor cooking. 2. Cooking, American. 3. Cooking—Ohio.
4. Tailgate parties. 5. Barbecuing. 6. Snack foods. 7. Ohio State
University—Miscellanea. 8. Ohio State Buckeyes (Football team—
Miscellanea. I. Metzler, Julie. II. Title.
TX823.E355 2013
641.59771—dc23
                                    2013003797

CONTENTS

Championship
CHICKEN WINGS

Ingredients

2 pounds chicken wings

1 teaspoon seasoned salt

$^1/_2$ teaspoon pepper

2 tablespoons hot sauce

2 tablespoons olive oil

2 cups flour

1 teaspoon garlic powder

$^1/_2$ cup butter

4 tablespoons brown sugar

$^1/_2$ cup maple syrup

3 teaspoons hot sauce

Makes 8–10 servings

Preheat the oven to 425 degrees. Prepare 2 baking sheets with aluminum foil and coat with nonstick cooking spray; set aside.

Divide the wings into the three jointed sections and discard the tips. Rinse and pat the wings dry using a paper towel and then put them into a large bowl. Add the seasoned salt, pepper, 2 tablespoons hot sauce, and olive oil and mix thoroughly until all of the wings are evenly coated.

In a gallon-size ziplock bag, add the flour and garlic powder and give it a few shakes to mix the ingredients. Add the wings to the bag in small batches and shake until the wings are evenly coated then transfer them to the prepared baking sheets. Repeat until all of the wings have been prepared. Spray each individual wing with cooking spray. Bake for 30 minutes then flip the wings over and bake for about 20 minutes more, or until juices run clear.

In the meantime, melt the butter in a medium saucepan on medium-low heat. Dissolve the brown sugar in the butter and add the maple syrup. Add 3 teaspoons hot sauce and simmer, stirring occasionally.

When the wings are done, remove from the oven and place in a large bowl. Pour the warm sauce over the wings and mix until all of the wings are evenly coated in the sauce; let rest for about 3 minutes for the sauce soak in. Place the wings on a serving tray, and serve with celery sticks, if desired.

Football
MEATBALLS

Ingredients

1 pound ground beef

$^1/_2$ cup plain breadcrumbs

1 egg

$^1/_2$ teaspoon salt

$^1/_8$ teaspoon seasoned salt

$^1/_2$ teaspoon pepper

$^1/_2$ teaspoon onion powder

$^1/_2$ teaspoon garlic powder

1 teaspoon dried parsley

**1 yellow onion, thinly
sliced, divided**

**1 cup barbecue sauce,
of choice, divided**

Makes 4 servings

Preheat the oven to 350 degrees. Tear off 4 (14-inch) sheets of aluminum foil and set aside.

In a large bowl, mix together the ground beef, breadcrumbs, egg, seasonings, and parsley. Form the mixture into 16 (1$^1/_2$-inch) balls. Place 4 meatballs onto each sheet of aluminum foil. Fold the sides up a little to prevent the toppings from spilling out and top each foil packet of meatballs with $^1/_4$ of the onion and $^1/_4$ cup barbecue sauce.

Gather the points of the foil together and lightly bunch them to make a sealed, funnel-shaped packet. Bake for 45 minutes and serve.

Dotting The "i"
DEVILED EGGS

Ingredients

12 hard-boiled eggs, cooled

**$1/2$ cup Miracle Whip
   Salad Dressing**

2 tablespoons mustard

Paprika

3 sweet pickle chips

Makes 12 servings

Peel and rinse the eggs then slice in half lengthwise. Scoop out the yolks and place them into a medium bowl. Mash the yolks with a fork, add the Miracle Whip and mustard, and beat until smooth.

Spoon the mixture into a plastic bag and cut off the tip of one of the corners, or use a pastry bag, if available. Place the egg whites on a serving tray and squeeze the yolk mixture through the open bag corner into the egg whites in a small circular pattern until full. Sprinkle paprika over the tops. Cut each of the pickle chips into quarters then place one quarter of the pickle gently into the top of each egg. Chill until ready to serve.

Field Goal
NACHOS

Ingredients

1 pound ground beef

$2/3$ cup water

**1 package (1 ounce)
taco seasoning mix**

**1 can (16 ounces) pinto
beans, drained**

**7 ounces restaurant-
style tortilla chips**

**6 ounces Nacho
Cheese Doritos**

$1/3$ cup taco sauce

1 cup grated cheddar cheese

**1 jar (15 ounces)
salsa con queso**

**1 cup grated pepper
jack cheese**

**2 cups grated Colby
Jack cheese**

2 green onions, chopped

Sour cream

Makes 12 servings

Preheat oven to 350 degrees.

In a large skillet, brown the beef and drain. Stir in the water, seasoning mix, and beans and cook until liquid is absorbed, about 5–7 minutes.

On a large baking sheet, mix the tortilla chips and the Doritos until uniformly distributed and then evenly layer on the taco sauce, cheddar cheese, beef and bean mixture, salsa con queso, pepper jack cheese, Colby Jack cheese, and green onions. Bake for 5 minutes, or until the cheeses are melted. Serve immediately with sour cream on the side.

Buckeye Nation
PIGS IN A BLANKET

Ingredients

1 package (14 ounces) Lit'l Smokies cocktail links

1 cup barbecue sauce, of choice

1/2 teaspoon Worcestershire sauce

1/2 teaspoon grape jelly

1 teaspoon packed brown sugar

2 teaspoons ketchup

1 can (8 ounces) crescent rolls

Makes 24 pieces

Place Lit'l Smokies, barbecue sauce, Worcestershire sauce, jelly, brown sugar, and ketchup into a medium saucepan and cook over medium-low heat, about 25–30 minutes, or until the sauce is thick and bubbly. Stir occasionally to keep the sauce from sticking to the bottom of the pan. Remove from heat and set aside.

Preheat oven to 375 degrees.

Unroll the crescent dough, cut each triangle lengthwise into thirds, and lay out, evenly spaced, onto an ungreased baking sheet. Using a fork, place one of the prepared Lit'l Smokies into each piece of crescent dough near the widest end. Roll up the links in the dough, ending with the point face down on the bottom. Bake for 13–15 minutes, or until golden. Remove from the oven and serve. You can use the leftover sauce for dipping.

The Silver Bullets
PEPPER JACK CHEESE STICKS

Ingredients

1 bag (10 ounces) pepper
jack cheese sticks

1 cup vegetable oil

$^1/_2$ cup flour

$^1/_4$ teaspoon salt

1 egg

1 tablespoon water

$^3/_4$ cup panko

$^1/_4$ teaspoon dried parsley

$^1/_4$ teaspoon coarsely
ground black pepper

Marinara or ranch
dip, optional

Makes 20 sticks

Unwrap the cheese sticks, cut in half vertically, and then place in a ziplock bag. Place the bag of cheese sticks into the freezer for at least 1 hour. Remove them after they have frozen and continue to the next step.

Heat the oil in a large skillet. Place a sheet of wax paper onto your work surface and place 3 shallow bowls onto it in a line. In the first bowl, combine the flour and salt. In the second bowl, beat the egg and stir in the water. In the third bowl, combine the panko, parsley, and pepper.

Once the oil is hot enough for frying, coat the cheese sticks in the seasoned flour, dip them into the egg mixture, and then quickly transfer them to the panko bowl, making sure that they are thoroughly coated in the panko flakes. Place them directly into the hot oil and fry for a total of about 3 minutes. Flip the cheese sticks after about 1 minute or when the bottoms are browned. Let the other side brown for another minute then fry the sides for about 30 seconds each. Remove from the oil and drain on paper towels. Serve immediately with dip of choice.

Columbus
QUESADILLAS

Ingredients

8 (10-inch) flour tortillas

4 slices American cheese

1 large tomato, diced, divided

1 package (8 ounces) smoked deli ham

1/2 teaspoon dried oregano, divided

2 cups grated sharp cheddar cheese

1 cup grated pepper jack cheese

Mayonnaise, optional

Red pepper hummus, optional

Makes 8–10 servings

Heat a large skillet over medium heat for about 3–5 minutes, or until the pan is hot.

Place 1 tortilla in the pan and put 1 slice of American cheese on top of it. Then layer on about 1/4 of the tomato, 4 slices ham, a sprinkle of oregano, 1/2 cup cheddar, and then 1/4 cup pepper jack. Place another tortilla on top and cook for about 5 minutes, or until the bottom tortilla is a golden color. Carefully flip the quesadilla over using a spatula, and cook for another 3–5 minutes, or until the bottom tortilla is golden and the cheese is melted through.

Remove from the skillet and let it rest for about a minute before slicing it in half then each of those halves into fourths. Repeat the process 3 more times.

Serve with mayo or red pepper hummus on the side.

Buckeye
CHOPS

Ingredients

1/2 red onion, chopped

4 cloves garlic, minced

1/4 cup Worcestershire sauce

1/2 teaspoon coarsely
   ground black pepper

1/4 teaspoon paprika

1/8 teaspoon crushed
   red pepper flakes

4 bone-in (3/4-inch-
   thick) pork chops

Makes 4 servings

In a small bowl, combine the onion, garlic, Worcestershire sauce, pepper, paprika, and red pepper to make a marinade. Place the pork chops into a large ziplock bag or covered dish and pour the marinade on top of them. Refrigerate for 4–8 hours.

Preheat grill.

Remove the pork chops from the refrigerator and discard the leftover marinade. Grill the pork chops over medium-hot fire for about 15–20 minutes, flipping once halfway through the cooking time. Remove the pork chops from the grill and let them rest for about 2–3 minutes then serve.

OSU Shredded
CHICKEN SANDWICHES

Ingredients

1 (3-pound) chicken, cooked, deboned, and shredded

3 $^1/_2$ cups chicken broth

2 cups quick 1-minute oats

$^3/_4$ cup plain breadcrumbs

2 $^1/_4$ teaspoons seasoned salt

$^1/_4$ teaspoon salt

$^1/_2$ teaspoon pepper

$^1/_4$ teaspoon seasoned pepper

$^1/_4$ teaspoon Morton's Nature's Seasons Seasoning Blend

20 hamburger buns

Colby cheese and sliced pickles, optional

Makes 18–20 sandwiches

Mix the chicken, broth, oats, breadcrumbs, and seasonings together in a slow cooker and cover. Cook on high for 3–4 hours or on low for 5–6 hours. Serve on hamburger buns, with cheese and pickle, if desired.

Tackle 'Em
TACO SOUP

Ingredients

1 pound boneless chicken breasts, cubed

32 ounces chicken broth

$^{1}/_{2}$ package taco seasoning

1 can (10 ounces) Rotel Tomatoes & Diced Green Chiles, with liquid

1 can (16 ounces) pinto beans, with liquid

1 bag (16 ounces) frozen yellow and white corn

4 ounces Velveeta cheese

1 bag (5 ounces) tortilla strips, optional

Tortilla corn chips

Makes about 8 servings

In a large, deep skillet or stockpot, boil the chicken in the broth until the chicken is fully cooked. Add in the taco seasoning, Rotel, pinto beans, and corn and stir until ingredients are thoroughly mixed. Cut the cheese into 1-inch cubes and stir them into the pot. Reduce heat and cover, stirring occasionally, until the cheese is melted and blended thoroughly with the rest of the ingredients.

Garnish with tortilla strips and serve with tortilla corn chips.

The Big "D"
RIBS

Ingredients

3 pounds boneless pork ribs

1/4 teaspoon seasoned salt, or to taste

2 cloves garlic, minced

1/2 medium onion, sliced into rings

1/2 teaspoon coarsely ground black pepper

1 1/2 tablespoons molasses

3 tablespoons Worcestershire sauce

1/4 cup barbecue sauce, of choice

3/4 cup root beer

Makes 6 servings

Place the ribs into a slow cooker and sprinkle with the seasoned salt. Add the garlic, onion, and pepper. Then add the molasses, Worcestershire sauce, barbecue sauce, and root beer. Cover and cook on low for about 8–9 hours or on high for 4–5 hours. Serve and enjoy.

O-H-I-O
BAKED ALFREDO

Ingredients

1 box (16 ounces)
   bow tie pasta

1 cup plus 2 tablespoons
   cornstarch, divided

2 tablespoons Italian
   seasoning, divided

2 teaspoons oregano, divided

1/4 teaspoon garlic powder

1/4 teaspoon onion powder

1/2 teaspoon salt, divided

1/4 teaspoon coarsely
   ground pepper, divided

1/4 cup olive oil

1 package (14 ounces)
   boneless, skinless
   chicken breast tenders

1 quart half-and-half

5 ounces freshly grated
   Parmesan cheese

1/2 cup grated sharp
   cheddar cheese

1/2 cup grated
   mozzarella cheese

Makes about 12 servings

Preheat oven to 350 degrees. Boil the pasta according to package instructions.

In the meantime, mix together 1 cup cornstarch, 1 tablespoon Italian seasoning, 1 teaspoon oregano, garlic powder, onion powder, 1/4 teaspoon salt, and 1/8 teaspoon pepper in a medium bowl. In a heavy skillet, heat oil on medium high. When the oil is hot, evenly coat the chicken tenders in the cornstarch mixture then place into the skillet. Fry the chicken for about 8–10 minutes on each side or until the middle is no longer pink. Take the chicken tenders out of the skillet and pat dry on paper towels then cut into 1-inch chunks and set aside.

Once the pasta is done, drain and transfer it into a 9 x 13-inch casserole dish. In the same saucepan as you used for the pasta, combine the half-and-half with the remaining seasonings. Cook over medium heat, stirring often to prevent scorching. Once hot, gradually add the Parmesan cheese, stirring continuously. It will boil quickly so keep stirring the bottom until it thickens. In a cup, mix remaining

cornstarch with about ¼ cup cold water to make
a thickener. Stir until smooth then gradually pour
into sauce, a little at a time, until desired thickness
occurs. Discard any unused thickener.

Add the chicken into the sauce and blend. Pour the
sauce over the pasta and stir until pasta is evenly
coated. Spread the cheddar and mozzarella cheeses
over the top and bake for 1 hour or until the sauce is
bubbly and the top layer of cheese is browned.

Brutus
BURGER SLIDERS

Burger Seasoning

1/2 teaspoon seasoned salt

1/4 teaspoon celery salt

1/4 teaspoon cracked pepper

1/4 teaspoon onion powder

1/8 teaspoon garlic powder

1 teaspoon dried parsley

Burgers

1 tablespoon butter

1 white onion, sliced

1 pound ground beef

2 ounces pepper jack cheese, grated

2 slices American cheese, cut into quarters

8 slider buns or Hawaiian bread rolls

1/2 pound bacon, cooked and drained

1/2 cup barbecue sauce, of choice

Makes 8 sliders

In a small bowl, combine the spices for the seasoning and mix well.

In a large skillet, melt the butter. Add onion and sauté for 5–7 minutes, or until the onion starts to caramelize, then transfer to a dish and set aside.

Divide the beef into 8 equal patties and sprinkle about 1/4 teaspoon of seasoning on each one. In the same skillet that the onions were cooked in, fry the burgers on medium heat for about 5 minutes on each side. Transfer to a plate. Add the onion back into the skillet and place the burgers on top. Add a sprinkle of pepper jack and a quarter slice of American cheese to the top of each burger. Cover the skillet to help with the melting process. Remove the burgers from heat.

Open a bun and place some onion on the bottom then add a burger patty, a strip of bacon, halved, and then about a teaspoon of barbecue sauce on the top bun. Return the top portion of the bun to the rest of the burger and enjoy.

Buckeye Grove
POTATO SOUP

Ingredients

4 ½ tablespoons
  butter, divided

½ white onion, diced

1 rib celery, diced

1 carrot, diced

2 cloves garlic, minced

¼ teaspoon salt

⅛ teaspoon pepper

8 ounces cooked cubed ham

32 ounces vegetable broth

1 tablespoon dried parsley

4 medium russet potatoes,
  peeled and cubed

2 ½ tablespoons flour

1 cup half-and-half

Grated sharp cheddar
  cheese, optional

Chopped scallions, optional

Makes about 8 servings

Melt 2 tablespoons butter in a large stockpot. Add the onion, celery, carrot, garlic, salt, and pepper and sauté for about 15 minutes. Add the ham and cook for about 5 more minutes. Then add the vegetable broth and parsley. Taste the broth at this point to see if it needs more salt. Add the potatoes to the stock. Cover and boil for about 15 minutes , or until the potatoes are cooked.

In the meantime, melt the remaining butter in a small saucepan over medium heat. Add the flour and stir continuously until the mixture forms a thick paste. Slowly add the half-and-half, stirring out all lumps before adding more. Stir continuously for about 5 minutes or until it becomes thick.

After the potatoes are cooked, add the half-and-half mixture to the soup while stirring continuously until well blended and soup is thickened. Heat for an additional 3–5 minutes and then serve. Garnish with cheese and scallions, if desired.

Victory Bell Veggie
PINWHEEL WRAPS

Ingredients

- **16 ounces cream cheese, softened**
- **1 cup mayonnaise (not Miracle Whip)**
- **1 package (1 ounce) dry ranch dip mix**
- **$2/3$ cup finely chopped mixed broccoli and cauliflower**
- **3 tablespoons finely chopped red bell pepper**
- **3 tablespoons finely chopped green bell pepper**
- **2 tablespoons shredded carrots**
- **2 tablespoons finely shredded cheddar jack cheese**
- **6 (10-inch) tomato and basil flour tortillas**

Makes 60 pieces

Mix the cream cheese, mayonnaise, ranch dip mix, vegetables, and cheese together in a medium bowl. Lay out 6 (12-inch) sheets of plastic wrap and then place the tortillas flat on top. Spoon about $1/2$ cup of the veggie mixture onto each tortilla. Start at one end and roll the tortillas up tightly, placing the end of each tortilla facedown on the plastic wrap. Fold the plastic wrap tightly around each tortilla and refrigerate for at least 2 hours. When ready to serve, remove from the plastic wrap and slice into 1-inch pieces. Arrange the veggie pinwheel wraps on a serving dish. This recipe is easily halved for smaller gatherings.

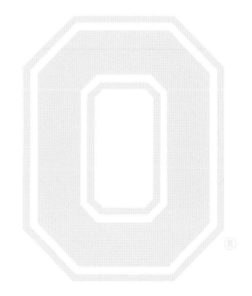

Gold Pants
POTATO PACKETS

Seasoning

1/4 teaspoon salt

1/8 teaspoon pepper

1/2 teaspoon garlic powder

1/4 teaspoon seasoned salt

1/8 teaspoon celery salt

1/2 teaspoon dried parsley

1/4 teaspoon dried thyme

Potato Packets

8 large red potatoes,
   washed and cut into
   1/4-inch chunks

1 medium yellow onion,
   sliced into rings

4 tablespoons butter

Makes 8 servings

Preheat grill. Combine the seasoning ingredients together in a small bowl and set aside.

Spread 8 (14-inch) pieces of aluminum foil on your work surface. Evenly divide the potato chunks between each piece of foil. Add 2–3 onion rings onto each pile of potatoes. Place 1/2 tablespoon butter onto each pile then sprinkle about 1/4 teaspoon of prepared seasoning over each mound of potatoes.

To make the packets, bring 2 opposite sides of the aluminum foil together and fold edges together, rolling until sealed on top. Then fold in the sides by creasing the edges and rolling until sealed. Do this for each packet. Get 8 more sheets of aluminum foil and place the sealed packets, crease down, on each one. Crease and fold edges around the packets, just like before. This creates a more insulated packet and stops the butter from leaking out.

Place packets on the top rack of a covered grill for about 10 minutes then turn and cook for another 10 minutes, or until the potatoes are soft. Remove from grill, open, and serve—either on a plate or leave in the individual packets.

The "O" Zone
GREEN BEAN CASSEROLE

Ingredients

2 tablespoons butter

8 ounces Baby Bella mushrooms, sliced

1 beef bouillon cube

$1/4$ cup hot water

$1/8$ teaspoon coarsely ground pepper

1 pint heavy whipping cream

2 tablespoons cornstarch

$1/2$ cup cold water

1 can (14.5 ounces) cut green beans, drained

1 can (14.5 ounces) French-cut green beans, drained

1 can (14.5 ounces) Italian-cut green beans, drained

1 $3/4$ cups French-fried onions

$3/4$ cup Fresh Gourmet Crispy Red Peppers

Makes 10–12 servings

Preheat oven to 350 degrees.

In a large skillet, melt the butter and add the mushrooms, sautéing over medium heat for about 5 minutes. Dissolve the bullion cube in the hot water and add to the mushrooms. Add the pepper and stir. Pour in the cream and stir until evenly blended. In a small bowl, mix the cornstarch into the cold water. While stirring continuously, add it to the cream mixture, a little at a time, until it reaches desired consistency.

Combine the green beans together in a 9 x 13-inch or a 2-quart casserole dish. Pour the creamed mushrooms over the green beans and bake for 50–55 minutes uncovered. Add fried onions around the outer edge of the casserole and the red peppers in the center. Raise the oven temperature to 375 degrees and bake an additional 5–7 minutes, or until topping is browned.

Buckeye Leaves
SALAD

Ingredients

1/2 cup plus 2 tablespoons olive oil, divided

1 package (3 ounces) ramen noodles, any flavor

2 tablespoons sunflower seeds

1/3 cup pistachios, shelled

1/3 cup sugar

1/3 cup vinegar

1/4 teaspoon Worcestershire sauce

1 head red leaf lettuce, torn into bite-size pieces

1 cup chopped broccoli

1/4 cup chopped green onions

2 ounces dried cranberries

Makes 10–12 servings

In a large skillet, heat 2 tablespoons of the oil over medium heat and crumble in the ramen noodles. Sauté for about 5 minutes, or until browned. Add in the sunflower seeds and pistachios and cook for another 5–7 minutes, stirring continuously to avoid burning. Turn off heat and remove from burner.

For the dressing, dissolve the sugar in the vinegar in a small bowl and then add the remaining oil and Worcestershire sauce. Mix until thoroughly blended.

Place the lettuce into a large bowl and add the broccoli, green onions, and dried cranberries, tossing until evenly distributed. Just before serving, add the ramen noodle mixture. Serve the dressing in a container on the side.

Block "O" Panko-
CRUSTED EGGPLANT

Ingredients

2 eggplants, peeled and cut into 1/2-inch-thick slices

1/2 teaspoon salt, divided

1 cup vegetable oil

1/2 cup flour

1/8 teaspoon pepper

1/4 teaspoon garlic powder

1/4 teaspoon onion powder

3 eggs

2 cups panko

1 teaspoon Italian seasoning

1/2 cup spaghetti sauce with mushrooms

1/2 cup grated mozzarella cheese

Dried parsley

Makes 24 slices

Preheat broiler. Line 2 baking sheets with aluminum foil and set aside. Place eggplant slices flat on a piece of wax paper and sprinkle with about 1/4 teaspoon of salt; set aside. Heat the oil in a large skillet.

In the meantime, lay down a sheet of wax paper and place 3 shallow bowls onto it in a line. In the first bowl, combine the flour, remaining salt, pepper, garlic powder, and onion powder. In the second bowl, beat the eggs. In the third bowl, combine the panko and Italian seasoning. Once the oil is hot enough for frying, coat the eggplant slices in the seasoned flour, then dip them into the eggs, and then quickly transfer them to the panko bowl, making sure that they are thoroughly coated in the panko flakes. Place them directly into the hot oil and fry for about 2 minutes on each side or until golden brown. Remove and drain on paper towels then transfer them to the prepared baking sheets in a single layer.

Spread about 1 teaspoon of spaghetti sauce on each eggplant slice, although a little less is needed for the smaller slices. Top each with a sprinkle of mozzarella cheese and parsley. Broil for about 2–3 minutes or until cheese begins to lightly brown. Remove the eggplant slices from the oven and serve.

Script "Ohio"
PASTA SALAD

Ingredients

12 ounces tri-color rotini pasta

2 packages (.6 ounces each) zesty Italian dressing mix

$1/4$ cup extra light olive oil

$1/2$ cup diced tomatoes

$1/2$ cup chopped broccoli florets

3 tablespoons grated Parmesan cheese

Makes 6–8 servings

Prepare the pasta according to package instructions to "al dente" firmness and then drain; set aside. In a small bowl, mix both packets of the dressing mix with the oil until well blended.

Place the pasta into a medium bowl and add the prepared dressing. Mix together until the pasta is thoroughly coated. Refrigerate for about an hour. After the pasta has chilled, stir in the broccoli and tomatoes. Garnish the top of pasta salad with the Parmesan cheese and serve.

TBDBITL
TACO DIP

Ingredients

1 pound ground beef

**1 package (1 ounce)
taco seasoning**

**1 can (16 ounces)
refried beans**

**1 jar (15.5 ounces)
white queso**

**6 sandwich slices
pepper jack cheese**

**3/4 cup grated sharp
cheddar cheese, divided**

**8 ounces gold and
white frozen corn**

**1 jar (15.5 ounces)
yellow queso**

3 to 4 ounces chunky salsa

Sour cream, optional

Makes about 12 cups

Preheat oven to 375 degrees.

In a large skillet, fry the beef and add the taco seasoning. Follow the cooking directions on the seasoning package.

Layer the ingredients in a 9 x 11-inch baking dish as follows: refried beans, white queso, 3 slices pepper jack, half of the cheddar cheese, corn, seasoned beef, yellow queso, 3 slices pepper jack, and the remaining cheddar cheese. Then add the salsa to the top in the center. Bake for 1 hour. Place the sour cream in a dish to the side.

Spirit Squad
SPINACH DIP

Ingredients

10 ounces frozen chopped spinach, thawed

8 ounces roasted red peppers, chopped

$1/4$ cup fresh parsley, minced

1 package (8 ounces) cream cheese, softened

1 cup prepared Alfredo sauce

1 cup grated Parmesan cheese

1 cup grated mozzarella cheese

1 teaspoon minced garlic

$1/4$ teaspoon pepper

Baked pita bread

Tortilla chips

Sesame dipping sticks

Makes 10–12 servings

Preheat oven to 350 degrees.

In a large bowl, mix together the spinach, red peppers, parsley, cream cheese, Alfredo sauce, cheeses, garlic, and pepper. Transfer the mixture to a 9 x 9-inch baking dish and bake for 25–30 minutes, or until the cheeses are melted and bubbly. Serve warm with baked pita bread, tortilla chips, and sesame dipping sticks.

Tunnel of Pride
FRENCH ONION DIP

Ingredients

2 cups sour cream

1 cup cream cheese, softened

$1/4$ teaspoon onion powder

$1/8$ teaspoon garlic powder

1 package (1 ounce) dry green onion dip mix

1 teaspoon chopped fresh chives

Potato chips

Crackers

Chopped vegetables

Makes 2 cups

Combine sour cream, cream cheese, onion powder, garlic powder, and dip mix in a medium bowl and blend until smooth. Garnish with chives. Cover and refrigerate for at least 30 minutes before serving. Serve with potato chips, crackers, and chopped vegetables.

Scarlet and Gray
HOT COCOA

Ingredients

2 teaspoons sugar

1 teaspoon unsweetened cocoa powder

4 ounces evaporated milk

4 ounces boiling water

Whipped cream

Red decorating sugar

Marshmallows, optional

Makes 1 cup

Place the sugar and cocoa in a large mug and mix them together. Add enough milk until the mug is about half full. Fill the rest with the boiling water and stir to combine. Add whipped cream and red decorating sugar or marshmallows, if desired.

"The Horseshoe"
SHERBET PUNCH

Ingredients

3 quarts raspberry sherbet

2 bottles (2 liters each) Sierra Mist

2 cups cranberry pomegranate juice

Place the sherbet in a large punch bowl. Pour the Sierra Mist over it and add in the cranberry pomegranate juice. Stir lightly and serve.

Makes 18–20 servings

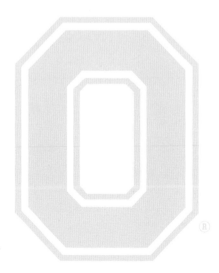

Ohio State
BUCKEYES

Ingredients

¹/₂ **cup butter**

³/₄ **cup creamy peanut butter**

2 ³/₄ **cups powdered sugar**

1 **(1-inch) square paraffin**

8 **ounces semisweet chocolate morsels**

Makes about 75 buckeyes

Melt the butter in the microwave in a large bowl. Add in the peanut butter and stir until blended. Add the powdered sugar, a little at a time, until thoroughly mixed. The dough should be very stiff. Place the dough in the freezer for about 15 minutes so the dough will stay smooth when rolling. Remove from freezer. Pinch off enough dough to roll into a ¹/₂-inch ball then place it on a baking sheet covered with wax paper. Repeat until all the dough has been rolled. Place the baking sheet into the freezer while preparing the chocolate.

Place the paraffin in the top of a double boiler or a small saucepan setting inside a deep skillet with about an inch of water in it. Melt the paraffin over a low to medium-low heat. After it has melted, add the chocolate morsels and stir.

Once the chocolate has started to melt, continuously stir the chocolate and paraffin until they are blended together. Stir the mixture occasionally until smooth and completely melted. Remove the peanut butter balls from the freezer and insert a toothpick into the top of one. Dip it into the chocolate and roll it on its side until the ball is coated, leaving the top of it uncoated, giving the candy a signature buckeye nut look. Take out the toothpick, use your finger to smooth over the hole where the toothpick was, and repeat for the rest of the tray. Return the Buckeyes to the freezer until ready to serve.

End Zone
CANDIED YAM CASSEROLE

Ingredients

4 large yams (or sweet potatoes)

$^1/_2$ cup butter

$^1/_2$ cup brown sugar

$^1/_4$ cup maple syrup

1 teaspoon cinnamon

$^3/_4$ teaspoon pumpkin pie spice

$^1/_2$ teaspoon sea salt

3 cups miniature marshmallows

Makes 4–6 servings

Preheat oven to 375 degrees. Peel the yams and cut into 1-inch chunks. Place in a large saucepan and boil for about 8–10 minutes until they are just underdone. Drain and transfer to a buttered deep baking dish; set aside.

In a small saucepan, melt the butter and stir in the brown sugar. Cook over medium heat, stirring until the brown sugar is completely dissolved. Add in the maple syrup, cinnamon, pumpkin pie spice, and salt. Cook and stir for about 3 minutes then pour the sauce over the yams. Gently mix until the yams are thoroughly coated. Cover and bake for 45 minutes, stirring about halfway through.

Remove the lid and add the marshmallows evenly over the top. Increase the oven temperature to 400 degrees and cook, uncovered, for 5–10 minutes, or until the marshmallows become lightly browned. Cover until ready to serve.

The Red Zone Velvet
SHORTBREAD COOKIES

Ingredients

1 cup softened butter

3/4 cup sugar

2 1/4 cups flour

2 teaspoons vanilla

2 tablespoons unsweetened cocoa powder

1 tablespoon red food coloring

1 teaspoon milk

1 container (16 ounces) cream cheese frosting

Red and black food coloring (paste food coloring works best for dark colors)

1 tube (4.25 ounces) red decorator frosting

1 tube (4.25 ounces) white decorator frosting

Makes about 24 cookies

Preheat the oven to 325 degrees. Place parchment paper on a baking sheet and set aside.

In a large bowl, cream the butter and sugar. Add the flour and knead with your hands to incorporate. Add the vanilla, cocoa powder, food coloring, and milk and knead until well blended. Place the dough on a lightly floured, flat surface. Roll the dough out evenly to 1/4 inch thick. Cut out the cookies with Ohio State cutters and place about an inch apart on the prepared baking sheet. Bake for 10–12 minutes. Transfer the cookies to a wire rack to cool.

Empty the container of frosting into a small bowl, or two small bowls if you want more than one color, and add food coloring to make the color you need; stir until blended. Decorate the cooled cookies by spreading the frosting on top and then use the decorator frosting to pipe on the details.

Buckeye Battle Cry
PUMPKIN PIE

Ingredients

1 cup sugar

1 teaspoon cinnamon

2 teaspoons pumpkin
   pie spice

2 teaspoons allspice

2 large eggs

1 can (12 ounces) pumpkin

1 teaspoon vanilla

1 can (12 ounces)
   evaporated milk

2 uncooked pie shells
   (9 inches each)

Whipped cream, optional

Cinnamon, optional

Makes 16 servings

Preheat oven to 375 degrees.

In a small bowl, mix together the sugar and spices;
set aside. In a large bowl, beat the eggs then mix in
the pumpkin. Add in the sugar mixture and vanilla
and stir until well blended. Pour in the milk and stir
until smooth.

Set the pie shells on a baking sheet. Evenly divide
the pumpkin mixture between them. Bake for
45 minutes to 1 hour. To check for doneness, insert
a toothpick or a knife into the center of the pie.
Pull it out, and if is clean, the pies are done. Let the
pies cool for a few minutes before slicing. Top with
whipped cream and a dusting of cinnamon, if desired.

Go Bucks!
TOFFEE NUTS

Ingredients

1 cup sugar

1 cup butter

3 tablespoons water

$^1/_2$ teaspoon cinnamon

1 teaspoon salt

1 $^1/_2$ cups cashews

1 $^1/_2$ cups almonds

Makes about 30 clusters

Combine the sugar, butter, water, cinnamon, and salt in a large, deep heavy-bottomed saucepan and cook on medium-high heat. Stir the mixture constantly to prevent scorching and bring to a boil. Using a candy thermometer, heat mixture to 280 degrees F then remove from heat. Immediately add the nuts and stir gently until well coated.

Pour the toffee nuts out onto a greased baking sheet and quickly form the nuts into clusters, about 1 inch in diameter. Allow the clusters to cool then serve.

ABOUT THE AUTHORS

Julie Metzler and Jen Elsner are sisters who enjoy sharing fun, food, and laughter. Julie graduated from The Ohio State University in 2001 with a degree in education. She has been teaching for 12 years, and is married with two daughters. Jen Elsner is a native Buckeye. She has a Master's Degree in Professional Writing from the University of Oklahoma and works for the University's English Department. She is also the author of *The University of Oklahoma Cookbook.*